Car Mania

RACE CARS

Ryan James

A Stingray Book

SEAHORSE PUBLISHING

Teaching Tips for Caregivers and Teachers:

This Hi-Lo book features high-interest subject matter that will appeal to all readers in intermediate and middle school grades. It may be enjoyed by students reading at or above grade level as well as by those who are looking for age-appropriate themes matched with a less challenging reading level. Hi-Lo books are ideal for ELL readers, too.

Each book appeals to a striving reader's age and maturity level. Opportunities are provided for students to read words they already know while encountering a limited number of new, high-interest vocabulary words. With these supports in place, students will read more fluently while increasing reading comprehension. Use the following suggestions to help students grow as readers.

- Encourage the student to read independently at home.
- Encourage the student to practice reading aloud.
- Encourage activities that require reading.
- Establish a regular reading time.
- Have the student write questions about what they read.

Teaching Tips for Teachers:

Before Reading

- Ask, "What do I know about this topic?"
- Ask, "What do I want to learn about this topic?"

During Reading

- Ask, "What is the author trying to teach me?"
- Ask, "How is this like something I already know?"

After Reading

- Discuss how the text features (headings, index, etc.) help with understanding the topic.
- Ask, "What interesting or fun fact did you learn?"

TABLE OF CONTENTS

WHAT IS A RACE CAR?

Race cars are built to go very fast and to have excellent performance.

Cutting-edge technology helps them win.

They are designed specifically for the type of race they will compete in. Some types of race cars are open-wheel, sports, stock, rally, and drag.

TOTAL
GEOX
INFINITI
Red Bull
TOTAL

THE FIRST CAR RACES

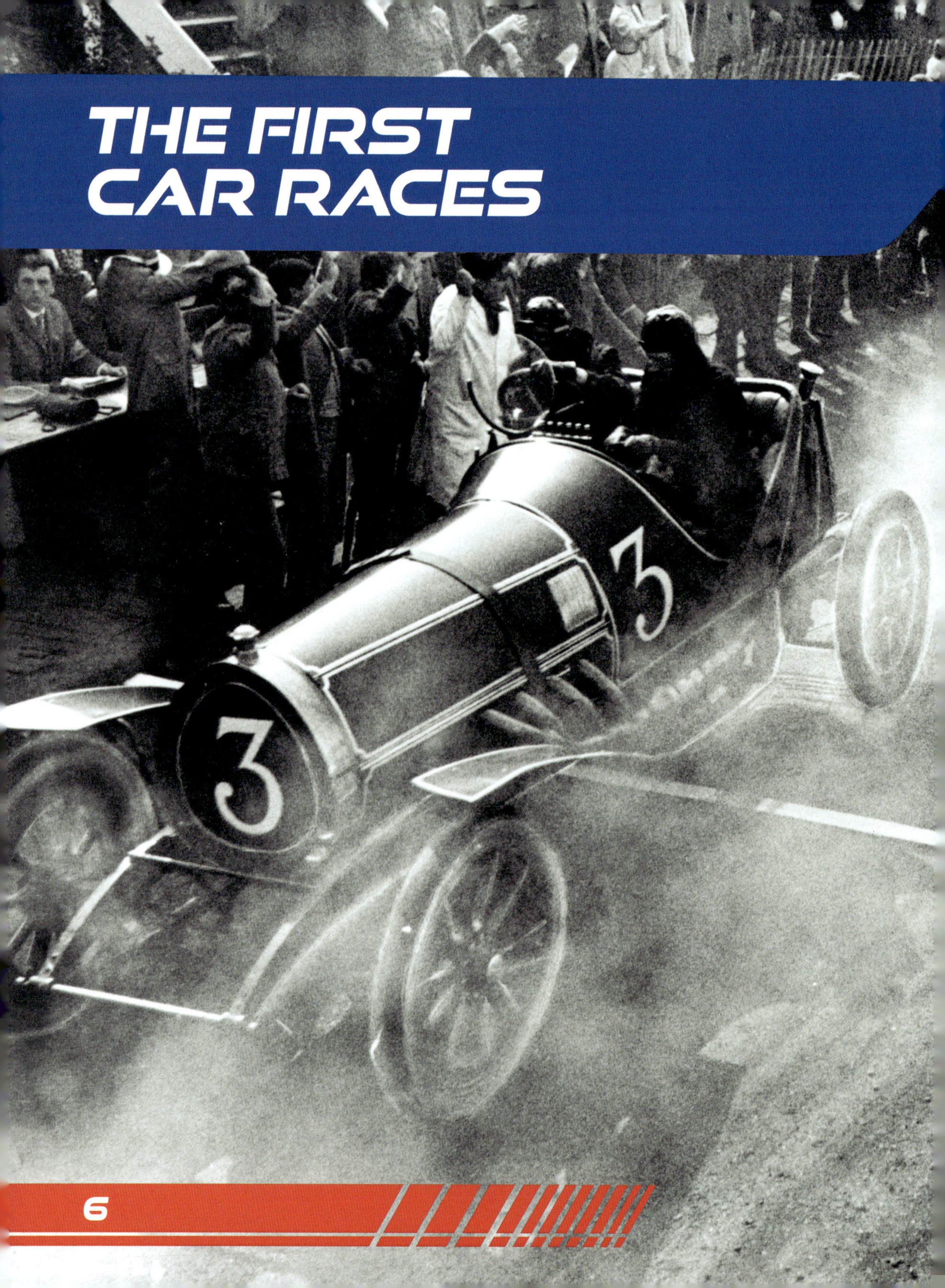

The first automobile race happened in the 1890s.

Racing was created soon after the invention of the gasoline-powered car.

In 1895, there was a race from Paris, France, to Bordeaux, France. Drivers used the streets through towns.

RACING ON TRACKS

During the 1930s, people near the Appalachian Mountains built fast cars and raced them on local tracks.

In 1947, Bill France Sr. created NASCAR (National Association for Stock Car Auto Racing).

Soon, races were held on specially created racetracks all over the United States.

FUN FACTS

The first NASCAR race was held on February 15, 1948, in Daytona Beach, Florida.

PARTS OF A RACE CAR

A race car has a cockpit where the driver sits.

Some cars have a **roll cage** to protect drivers.

Special tires increase **traction** on the road.

Some race car engines can reach speeds of 320 miles (515 kilometers) per hour.

FORMULA RACERS

The most expensive and **prestigious** race cars are open-wheel cars.

Most have just one seat, and the wheels are set outside the car's main body.

These cars are used for formula racing.

Drivers need to be highly skilled at this level of racing.

FUN FACTS

Formula race cars can run upside-down in tunnels as they go 120 miles (193 kilometers) per hour.

SPORTS RACERS

Sports cars are often used in races.

They are similar to regular cars, but they have **enhanced** engines and other features.

The technology used in sports cars today may appear in the ordinary cars of the future.

Customers can buy Grand Touring (GT) cars that look like high-performing race cars.

STOCK RACERS

Stock cars are used in NASCAR races.

The roofs, hoods, and trunks must be **stock** parts.

The bodies for stock cars must match a strict **template**.

Chevrolet, Ford, and Toyota build stock cars from sedans they make for the road.

FUN FACTS

When going 200 miles (322 kilometers) per hour, stock cars can cover the length of a football field in one second.

RALLY AND DRAG RACERS

Rally cars are regular cars that are **modified** to handle driving through mud, sand, dirt, and snow. Good tires and **suspensions** help tackle tough ground.

Cars for drag racing are designed to reach high speeds quickly for short distances.

No matter the type, race cars are built for speed!

TOP MODELS

NASCAR

Chevrolet Camaro ZL1

Top driver: Chase Elliott

Top speed: 202 mph (325 kph)

Horsepower: 650

Toyota Camry TRD

Top driver: Martin Truex Jr.

Top speed: 135 mph (217 kph)

Horsepower: 301

Ford Mustang

Top driver: Ryan Blaney

Top speed: 163 mph (262 kph)

Horsepower: 410

FORMULA 1

Mercedes-AMG Project One

Top driver: Lewis Hamilton

Top speed: 217 mph (349 kph)

Horsepower: 1,000

Red Bull RB13

Top driver: Max Verstappen

Top speed: 215 mph (346 kph)

Horsepower: 900

McLaren 570S

Top driver: Lando Norris

Top speed: 204 mph (328 kph)

Horsepower: 562

GLOSSARY

enhanced (en-HANSD): made bigger, better, or more attractive

modified (MAH-duh-fyed): changed to meet a specific need

prestigious (pres-TIJ-uhs): highly respected, successful, powerful, or famous

roll cage (rohl kayj): a special framework of metal bars encasing the driver of a vehicle

stock (stahk): regularly available for anyone to buy

suspensions (suh-SPEN-shuhnz): systems of car parts that have springs to make the car stable, protecting it from the road and helping the driver maintain control

template (TEM-plit): a guide with specifications for building or making something

traction (TRAK-shuhn): the force that keeps a moving body from slipping on a surface, such as a moving tire on a road

INDEX

AFTER READING QUESTIONS

1. In what country was the first automobile race held?
2. What parts of NASCAR cars must be stock items?
3. On what kinds of tracks do rally cars race?
4. Describe open-wheel cars.
5. Name three things that could help protect race car drivers.

ABOUT THE AUTHOR

Ryan James lives in Western North Carolina with his dog Bailey. His favorite race to watch is the Daytona 500. His dream is to own a Lamborghini. When he's not writing books, you can find him backpacking through Pisgah Forest, North Carolina.

Written by: Ryan James
Design by: Kathy Walsh
Editor: Kim Thompson

Library of Congress PCN Data
Race Cars / Ryan James
Car Mania
ISBN 978-1-63897-473-4 (hard cover)
ISBN 978-1-63897-588-5 (paperback)
ISBN 978-1-63897-703-2 (EPUB)
ISBN 978-1-63897-818-3 (eBook)
Library of Congress Control Number: 2022933103

Printed in the United States of America.

Seahorse Publishing Company
www.seahorsepub.com

Published in the United States
Seahorse Publishing
PO Box 771325
Coral Springs, FL 33077

SEAHORSE PUBLISHING